AI Disclaimer

The information presented in "Smart Strategies for Low-Risk High Yield Stocks in 2025" is for educational and informational purposes only. While the strategies and insights provided are based on research and analysis available up to October 2023, investing in the stock market involves significant risks, and past performance is not indicative of future results. This book does not constitute financial, investment, or legal advice. Readers are encouraged to conduct their own research and consult with a qualified financial advisor before making any investment decisions. The authors and publishers of this book are not responsible for any losses or damages arising from the use of the information contained herein. Investment strategies discussed in this book may not be suitable for all investors. Individual circumstances, risk tolerance, and market conditions can vary widely. Therefore, any decision to act upon the information provided is strictly at your own risk. Additionally, while artificial intelligence and other technological tools have been utilized in the analysis and development of the content, the insights generated should not be considered infallible. The financial landscape is constantly evolving, and the application of AI in investment strategies is an emerging field subject to change. By reading this book, you acknowledge and agree to these terms.

Table Of Contents

Chapter 2: Dividend Aristocrats 2
Chapter 3: ESG Investing 2
Chapter 4: Blue-Chip Stocks 2
Chapter 5: REITs (Real Estate Investment Trusts) 2
Chapter 6: Growth at a Reasonable Price (GARP) 2
Chapter 7: Defensive Stocks 2
Chapter 8: International High-Yield Stocks 2
Chapter 9: Technology Dividends 2
Chapter 10: Sector Rotation Strategies 2
Chapter 11: Low-Volatility ETFs 2
Chapter 12: Conclusion 2
Chapter 1: Introduction to Low-Risk High-Yield Investing 1

Chapter 1: Introduction to Low-

Risk High-Yield Investing

Understanding Low-Risk and High-Yield

Understanding low-risk and high-yield investments is crucial for investors seeking to optimize their portfolios in 2025. Low-risk investments typically offer more stability and predictability in returns, while high-yield investments aim to maximize income through dividends or interest. The ideal strategy combines these two elements, allowing investors to enjoy substantial returns without exposing their capital to excessive risk. This approach is particularly relevant in today's volatile market, where economic uncertainties necessitate a careful selection of investment opportunities.

One effective strategy for identifying low-risk, high-yield stocks is to focus on Dividend Aristocrats. These are companies with a proven track record of consistently increasing their dividends over many years. Such businesses often possess strong fundamentals and a stable revenue base, making them less susceptible to economic downturns. By investing in Dividend Aristocrats, investors can benefit from regular income payments while also experiencing potential capital appreciation. This dual benefit makes them an attractive option for those looking to balance risk and reward.

Environmental, social, and governance (ESG) investing has gained traction among investors aiming for sustainable returns. Companies that prioritize ESG criteria often demonstrate lower risk profiles due to their focus on ethical practices and long-term sustainability. These firms are increasingly recognized for their ability to generate steady returns while mitigating risks associated with regulatory changes or reputational damage. By integrating ESG factors into their investment strategy, stock market investors can align their financial goals with their values, leading to both ethical and profitable investment choices.

Blue-chip stocks represent another viable avenue for low-risk, high-yield investments. These established companies are typically leaders in their respective industries, with a history of strong performance and reliability. Investing in blue-chip stocks can provide a sense of security, as these firms tend to weather economic fluctuations better than their smaller counterparts. Furthermore, many blue-chip companies offer dividends, enhancing their appeal for income-focused investors. By including these stocks in their portfolios, investors can achieve a balanced approach between growth and income generation.

Real Estate Investment Trusts (REITs) also present an attractive option for those seeking consistent income with lower volatility. REITs invest in income-generating real estate and are required to distribute a significant portion of their earnings as dividends. This structure allows investors to gain exposure to the real estate market without the complexities of direct property ownership. Additionally, REITs can provide diversification benefits, as their performance often correlates differently from traditional stocks. By incorporating REITs into their investment strategies, investors can enhance their income streams while managing risk effectively.

The Importance of Diversification

Diversification is a foundational principle in investment strategy, particularly for those seeking to navigate the complexities of the stock market in 2025. By spreading investments across a variety of asset classes, sectors, and geographic regions, investors can mitigate risk while still capitalizing on potential returns. In an era marked by volatility and rapid technological advancement, the need for a diversified portfolio is more pronounced than ever. This approach not only buffers against market downturns but also positions investors to take advantage of growth opportunities across different sectors, such as technology, ESG, and international markets.

One of the key benefits of diversification is its ability to reduce unsystematic risk, which is the risk inherent to a specific company or industry. By investing in a blend of stocks, including Dividend Aristocrats and blue-chip companies, investors can safeguard their portfolios from the adverse effects of a downturn in any single sector. For instance, while the tech industry may experience significant fluctuations, sectors like utilities or consumer staples often provide stability during economic downturns. This balance of high-risk and low-risk investments can lead to a more resilient portfolio that withstands market fluctuations.

Moreover, diversification allows investors to explore various niches, such as REITs and low-volatility ETFs, which can offer consistent income with lower volatility. Real estate investments through REITs can be an effective way to gain exposure to a different asset class that behaves independently of stock market trends. Similarly, low-volatility ETFs focus on stocks that have historically exhibited steadier price movements, providing a cushion against market volatility. By incorporating these investment vehicles, investors can enhance their portfolios' stability while still pursuing growth.

Another aspect of diversification is the opportunity to engage in strategies like Growth at a Reasonable Price (GARP) and sector rotation. GARP enables investors to identify undervalued stocks that possess strong growth potential, while sector rotation allows them to allocate funds based on the economic cycle. By understanding which sectors are likely to outperform at any given time, investors can optimize their returns while managing risk. This strategic allocation becomes crucial in a fast-changing economic landscape, where sectors such as clean energy and technology are poised for substantial growth.

Finally, international diversification should not be overlooked. By investing in international high-yield stocks, investors can access foreign markets that offer attractive dividend yields with manageable risk. This global perspective not only enhances potential returns but also reduces the impact of domestic economic downturns. In 2025, as the world becomes increasingly interconnected, embracing a diversified approach that spans geographic boundaries and sectors will be essential for stock market investors, brokers, and those engaged in niche markets like crypto, EV vehicles, and space exploration.

Overview of Investment Strategies for 2025

The investment landscape for 2025 presents a range of strategies tailored to meet the needs of diverse investors. As stock market dynamics evolve, investors must adapt their approaches to achieve sustainable growth while minimizing risk. Key strategies include identifying Dividend Aristocrats, which are companies with a history of increasing dividends. These companies not only provide a steady income stream but also demonstrate resilience during economic downturns, making them an essential component of a low-risk, high-yield portfolio.

ESG investing continues to gain traction as investors increasingly prioritize socially responsible and environmentally sustainable companies. This strategy aligns financial objectives with ethical considerations, focusing on firms that maintain solid returns while adhering to responsible practices. Investing in ESG-compliant companies can mitigate risks associated with regulatory changes and reputational damage, presenting a compelling option for those looking to balance profit with purpose.

Blue-chip stocks are another cornerstone of low-risk investing. These established companies have a proven track record of reliability and strong performance, making them attractive to conservative investors. By focusing on blue-chip stocks, investors can benefit from the stability of large, well-managed firms that are less susceptible to market volatility. This strategy not only provides potential capital appreciation but also often includes dividends that enhance overall returns.

Real Estate Investment Trusts (REITs) offer an alternative avenue for income generation with lower volatility. REITs allow investors to gain exposure to real estate markets without the complexities of direct property ownership. They typically distribute a significant portion of their earnings as dividends, making them an appealing choice for income-focused investors. Additionally, growth at a reasonable price (GARP) combines the principles of growth investing with value, allowing investors to identify undervalued stocks with potential for appreciation, adding a layer of strategic depth to their portfolios.

Finally, low-volatility exchange-traded funds (ETFs) represent a prudent choice for investors seeking stability amidst market fluctuations. These funds focus on stocks with lower price volatility, providing steady returns over time. Sector rotation strategies can further enhance portfolio performance by reallocating investments based on economic cycles, targeting sectors that show promise during different market conditions. By embracing a diversified approach that includes these strategies, investors can position themselves for success in the evolving landscape of 2025.

Chapter 2: Dividend Aristocrats

Identifying Dividend Aristocrats

Identifying Dividend Aristocrats involves a meticulous analysis of companies that have not only survived through various economic cycles but have also consistently increased their dividends for at least 25 consecutive years. These companies represent a rare breed of stocks that blend reliability with income generation, making them highly attractive for investors seeking low-risk, high-yield opportunities. To qualify as a Dividend Aristocrat, a company must demonstrate strong financial health, a commitment to returning value to shareholders, and a robust business model that can weather economic fluctuations. Investors should begin by examining a company's dividend history, payout ratios, and earnings growth to determine if it meets the criteria for long-term dividend stability.

The significance of Dividend Aristocrats extends beyond their dividend payments; these companies are often blue-chip stocks that reflect resilience in both stable and volatile markets. Their established positions in their respective industries allow them to maintain profitability even during downturns. This stability not only attracts conservative investors but also serves as a hedge against market volatility. By focusing on these stalwarts, investors can create a more secure portfolio that balances growth potential with income stability, which is particularly beneficial for those navigating the complex landscape of 2025's stock market.

In addition to traditional metrics, understanding the broader economic context is essential when identifying Dividend Aristocrats. Factors such as interest rates, inflation, and global economic conditions can significantly impact a company's ability to sustain and grow dividends. Investors should consider both macroeconomic indicators and sector-specific trends. For instance, sectors like consumer staples and utilities tend to be more resilient during economic downturns, making companies within these sectors appealing candidates for dividend aristocracy. By adopting a comprehensive market analysis approach, investors can better position themselves to identify companies that not only have a history of dividend growth but also the potential for continued success.

ESG investing is increasingly important in today's investment landscape, particularly as more investors seek to align their portfolios with their values. Dividend Aristocrats that prioritize environmental, social, and governance criteria not only appeal to socially conscious investors but also tend to exhibit lower volatility and risk. Companies that invest in sustainable practices and ethical governance are often better positioned for long-term growth, as they can attract a loyal customer base and mitigate risks associated with regulatory changes. This intersection of ESG and dividend growth creates a compelling opportunity for investors aiming for both income and impact.

Lastly, diversifying investments through international high-yield stocks and sector rotation strategies can enhance the appeal of Dividend Aristocrats. By identifying global companies with a strong track record of dividend payments, investors can capitalize on high yields while managing risk. Additionally, employing sector rotation strategies allows investors to allocate funds to Dividend Aristocrats that may be positioned to outperform based on economic cycles. Combining these strategies with a focus on low-volatility ETFs can further optimize returns while minimizing risk, ultimately leading to a robust investment portfolio that thrives in the evolving market landscape of 2025.

Evaluating Dividend Growth and Stability

Evaluating dividend growth and stability is essential for investors seeking reliable income streams in a fluctuating market. A key aspect of this evaluation involves identifying Dividend Aristocrats, which are companies that have consistently increased their dividends for 25 consecutive years or more. These companies not only exhibit a commitment to returning value to shareholders but also demonstrate resilience in their business models. For investors looking for low-risk, high-yield opportunities, Dividend Aristocrats often represent a solid foundation, as their long-standing history of dividend growth reflects both stability and financial health.

Another critical component of evaluating dividend growth is the assessment of Environmental, Social, and Governance (ESG) factors. Companies that prioritize ESG principles tend to attract more investment and often exhibit greater stability. By focusing on firms that are committed to sustainable practices, investors can identify those that not only provide solid returns but also align with their values. As ESG investing gains traction, firms with strong ESG profiles are likely to experience enhanced dividend growth, making them attractive options for low-risk portfolios.

Blue-chip stocks further contribute to the landscape of dividend growth and stability. These are well-established companies with a proven track record of reliability and performance, typically characterized by strong balance sheets and consistent cash flow. Investing in blue-chip stocks allows investors to benefit from steady dividend payouts while minimizing risk. These companies often have the financial strength to weather economic downturns, ensuring that dividends remain intact even during challenging market conditions.

Real Estate Investment Trusts (REITs) represent another avenue for consistent income through dividends. By investing in REITs, investors can access a diversified portfolio of real estate assets that generate rental income, which is then distributed to shareholders in the form of dividends. This can provide a stable income stream with lower volatility compared to traditional stocks. REITs can be particularly appealing for those looking to balance their portfolios with investments that offer regular payouts and exposure to real estate markets.

Lastly, the concept of Growth at a Reasonable Price (GARP) is crucial for evaluating dividend growth potential. GARP investing combines elements of both growth and value investing, focusing on stocks that are not only priced attractively but also have solid growth prospects. By identifying undervalued stocks poised for growth, investors can capitalize on dividends that may increase as these companies expand. This strategy, along with sector rotation and low-volatility ETFs, allows investors to navigate various market cycles effectively while maintaining a focus on dividend stability and growth.

Case Studies of Successful Dividend Aristocrats

Examining successful Dividend Aristocrats reveals valuable insights for investors seeking stable, high-yield income streams. Dividend Aristocrats are companies that have increased their dividends for at least 25 consecutive years, demonstrating resilience and a commitment to returning value to shareholders. One notable example is Procter & Gamble, a leader in consumer staples. Its diversified product portfolio and global reach have allowed it to maintain steady revenue streams, even in economic downturns. This stability has facilitated consistent dividend growth, making it a prime candidate for investors looking for reliable income.

Another exemplary Dividend Aristocrat is Coca-Cola, which has a long-standing reputation for delivering dividends. The company's strong brand recognition and extensive distribution network have positioned it well to weather economic fluctuations. Coca-Cola's ability to adapt its product offerings to changing consumer preferences, such as introducing healthier beverage options, has allowed it to sustain its dividend increases. This adaptability is crucial for investors focusing on companies with a proven track record of resilience and innovation, particularly in sectors like consumer goods.

3M is also a noteworthy case study among Dividend Aristocrats. With its diversified operations across various industries, including healthcare, consumer products, and industrial goods, 3M has managed to remain robust even amidst market volatility. The company's commitment to research and development has led to innovative products that meet evolving customer needs. This focus on innovation, combined with a stable dividend history, positions 3M as an attractive option for investors looking for a blend of safety and growth potential.

In the technology sector, Microsoft stands out as a Dividend Aristocrat that balances growth and income. The company's transformation from a software giant to a leader in cloud computing has driven significant revenue growth, allowing it to return capital to shareholders through regular dividend increases. Microsoft's focus on sustainable business practices and its commitment to ESG principles resonate with investors prioritizing socially responsible investing. This alignment with modern investment strategies enhances Microsoft's appeal as a long-term investment option.

Lastly, Johnson & Johnson exemplifies a Dividend Aristocrat with a strong commitment to healthcare innovation and consumer products. Its diversified business model and global presence enable it to navigate economic uncertainties effectively. Johnson & Johnson's consistent dividend growth reflects its robust financial health and the strategic management of its product lines. For investors seeking low-risk, high-yield opportunities, Johnson & Johnson offers a compelling case for inclusion in a balanced investment portfolio, particularly in a landscape increasingly focused on stability and consistent returns.

Chapter 3: ESG Investing

Principles of ESG Investing

Principles of ESG Investing emphasize the integration of environmental, social, and governance factors into investment decisions. This approach is gaining traction among stock market investors, brokers, and various niche investors, including those involved in technology, renewable energy, and even traditional sectors like oil and gas. The foundation of ESG investing lies in the belief that companies committed to sustainable practices and ethical governance tend to outperform their peers over the long term, thereby offering investors solid returns with lower associated risks.

By focusing on businesses that prioritize environmental stewardship, social responsibility, and sound governance, investors can align their portfolios with personal values while seeking financial growth.

One of the key principles of ESG investing is the environmental aspect, which evaluates a company's impact on the planet. This includes factors such as carbon emissions, waste management, resource use, and overall ecological impact. Investors are increasingly scrutinizing companies for their environmental practices, especially in industries like fossil fuels and EV batteries, where sustainability is crucial.

Companies that proactively address their environmental footprint not only contribute positively to global sustainability efforts but also mitigate risks associated with regulatory penalties and public backlash, making them more appealing to risk-averse investors.

The social dimension of ESG investing focuses on a company's relationships with its stakeholders, including employees, customers, suppliers, and communities. This principle emphasizes the importance of fair labor practices, diversity and inclusion, and community engagement. Investors are recognizing that companies that prioritize social responsibility tend to cultivate loyal customer bases and maintain strong reputations, ultimately leading to better financial performance. In sectors such as technology and sports, where public perception plays a significant role, companies that excel in social governance are often better positioned for long-term growth.

Governance is the third pillar of ESG investing and pertains to a company's leadership, internal controls, and shareholder rights. Strong governance structures ensure that companies are managed effectively, transparently, and ethically. Investors are increasingly looking for companies with diverse boards, robust risk management practices, and accountability measures. By investing in firms with strong governance frameworks, investors can reduce the risk of corporate scandals, mismanagement, and other issues that can negatively impact stock performance. This focus on governance is particularly relevant for investors in high-yield sectors, where the potential for higher returns must be balanced with a thorough assessment of corporate integrity.

Incorporating ESG principles into investment strategies is not just a moral or ethical choice; it is also a strategic one that aligns with the growing trend of socially responsible investing. As more investors recognize the financial benefits of targeting companies that adhere to ESG criteria, the demand for such investments continues to rise. This shift presents opportunities for various niches, from tech and cryptocurrency to real estate and defensive stocks. By prioritizing ESG factors, investors can enhance their portfolios with high-yield, low-risk stocks that not only promise financial returns but also contribute positively to society and the environment, paving the way for a sustainable investment future.

Evaluating ESG Metrics

Evaluating ESG metrics is critical for investors seeking to align their portfolios with environmentally and socially responsible practices while securing solid returns. Environmental, Social, and Governance (ESG) criteria assess a company's resilience to long-term risks and its ability to generate sustainable financial performance. For stock market investors, particularly those focused on low-risk, high-yield opportunities, understanding these metrics is essential in identifying companies that not only perform well financially but also contribute positively to society and the environment.

One of the primary components of ESG evaluation is environmental metrics, which measure a company's impact on the planet. Investors should look for companies with robust strategies for reducing carbon emissions, waste management, and resource conservation. As the global economy shifts towards sustainability, firms that prioritize these initiatives are more likely to thrive and appeal to a growing base of environmentally-conscious consumers. This positions them favorably in the market, potentially leading to higher stock valuations and dividends over time.

Social metrics assess how a company manages relationships with its employees, suppliers, customers, and the communities in which it operates. Key indicators include workforce diversity, employee satisfaction, and community engagement. Companies that excel in these areas often experience lower turnover rates and stronger brand loyalty, translating into more stable financial performance. For investors, particularly those targeting sectors like technology and consumer goods, prioritizing firms with strong social metrics can mitigate risks associated with reputational damage and regulatory scrutiny.

Governance metrics focus on a company's leadership, executive pay, audits, internal controls, and shareholder rights. Strong governance practices ensure that companies operate transparently and ethically, reducing the likelihood of fraud and mismanagement. Investors should seek companies with diverse boards of directors and transparent decision-making processes. These attributes can lead to more prudent management practices and enhance overall corporate performance, making such firms attractive for investment, especially in volatile market conditions where stability is paramount.

Incorporating ESG metrics into investment strategies can also lead to superior financial returns. Research indicates that companies with strong ESG practices often outperform their peers, particularly in challenging economic environments. By diversifying portfolios to include high-quality ESG-compliant companies, investors can benefit from both financial gains and the fulfillment of contributing to sustainable development. As the investment landscape evolves, embracing ESG metrics will not only align with ethical considerations but also enhance portfolio resilience and long-term profitability.

Top ESG Stocks for 2025

As we look towards 2025, the investment landscape for ESG (Environmental, Social, and Governance) stocks is becoming increasingly attractive to a diverse range of investors. Companies that prioritize sustainable practices and ethical governance not only contribute positively to society but also present a compelling investment opportunity. For stock market investors and brokers, identifying top ESG stocks can yield high returns while minimizing risk, aligning with the broader trend of socially responsible investing. This shift is not just a passing fad; it reflects a fundamental change in how investors evaluate potential stocks.

Among the leading candidates for ESG investment are established companies known for their commitment to sustainability. These businesses typically belong to the Dividend Aristocrats category, demonstrating a long-standing history of increasing dividends while maintaining stability. Companies in sectors such as renewable energy, sustainable agriculture, and green technology are poised to benefit from the growing emphasis on sustainability. Investors should focus on these firms, as they not only promise steady income through dividends but also show potential for capital appreciation driven by increasing consumer preference for eco-friendly products and services.

Blue-chip stocks are another critical area of focus within the ESG space. These companies are well-established, financially sound, and have a proven track record of reliability and performance. Many blue-chip firms are increasingly adopting sustainable practices and enhancing their ESG profiles, making them attractive options for investors seeking lower-risk opportunities. By investing in these stocks, investors can enjoy the benefits of a stable investment while supporting companies that prioritize ethical practices and social responsibility, aligning financial goals with personal values.

Real Estate Investment Trusts (REITs) that focus on sustainable properties also present an intriguing opportunity for ESG-conscious investors. These REITs often invest in eco-friendly buildings and developments that meet high environmental standards. As the demand for sustainable real estate continues to grow, these investments can provide consistent income with lower volatility. For those looking to diversify their portfolios, exploring REITs that emphasize ESG criteria can enhance the overall stability of their investment strategy while contributing to a more sustainable future.

Finally, the Growth at a Reasonable Price (GARP) strategy can be effectively applied to the ESG sector. This approach combines growth investing with value principles, helping investors identify undervalued stocks that are poised for growth while maintaining a commitment to sustainability. By focusing on companies that meet both ESG criteria and possess strong growth potential, investors can position themselves to capitalize on the dual benefits of financial returns and positive societal impact. In an era where responsible investing is gaining momentum, identifying top ESG stocks for 2025 will be paramount for those aiming to achieve high yields with low risk.

Chapter 4: Blue-Chip Stocks

Characteristics of Blue-Chip Companies

Blue-chip companies are recognized for their stability, reliability, and strong financial performance, making them a cornerstone of many investment portfolios. These companies typically have a long history of success, established market leadership, and a track record of generating consistent revenue and profits. Investors are drawn to blue-chip stocks not only for their potential for capital appreciation but also for their ability to provide regular dividends, which can be reinvested or used as a source of income. Their established presence in the market often allows them to weather economic downturns better than smaller, less established companies.

One defining characteristic of blue-chip companies is their robust market capitalization, usually exceeding several billion dollars. This size provides them with the financial resources to invest in research and development, expand their operations, and navigate economic challenges. For stock market investors, this means that blue-chip stocks often represent less risk compared to smaller firms, as larger companies tend to have diversified revenue streams and a more extensive customer base. This diversification is particularly appealing in volatile markets, where smaller companies may struggle to maintain stability.

Another hallmark of blue-chip companies is their commitment to returning value to shareholders through dividends. Many of these companies are known as Dividend Aristocrats, consistently increasing their dividends for decades. This history of dividend growth is a testament to their strong cash flow and management's commitment to rewarding investors. For income-focused investors, such as those interested in defensive stocks or REITs, blue-chip dividends provide a reliable stream of income, aligning with the strategy of investing in stocks that offer both growth potential and stability.

Blue-chip companies also tend to prioritize sound governance and ethical business practices, aligning with the principles of ESG investing. These companies often implement sustainable business practices that not only benefit the environment and society but also enhance their operational efficiency and profitability. This focus on corporate responsibility can mitigate risks associated with regulatory changes and reputational damage, appealing to investors who seek to balance financial returns with ethical considerations in their investment strategies.

Finally, blue-chip stocks often play a crucial role in sector rotation strategies. Their stability allows investors to pivot between sectors based on economic conditions while maintaining a core position in reliable companies. For those interested in growth at a reasonable price, blue-chip companies can present opportunities to invest in established businesses that are still poised for growth. As the market evolves, blue-chip stocks offer a low-risk, high-yield investment avenue, making them an essential consideration for anyone looking to build a resilient and profitable investment portfolio in 2025.

Analyzing Performance Metrics

Analyzing performance metrics is crucial for stock market investors seeking to optimize their portfolios in 2025. Understanding these metrics allows investors to gauge the health and potential of various stocks, particularly in sectors like technology, renewable energy, and traditional industries. Metrics such as earnings per share (EPS), price-to-earnings (P/E) ratio, dividend yield, and return on equity (ROE) provide insights into a company's operational efficiency and profitability. By focusing on these key indicators, investors can make informed decisions about allocating resources to high-paying, low-risk stocks, such as Dividend Aristocrats, which offer both stability and reliable returns.

For those interested in ESG investing, performance metrics take on additional significance. Companies that prioritize environmental, social, and governance criteria often report on sustainability metrics, which can be a vital part of their performance evaluations. Metrics such as carbon footprint reduction, employee diversity, and community engagement scores not only reflect a company's commitment to responsible practices but can also indicate long-term viability and profitability. Investors should analyze these metrics in conjunction with traditional financial indicators to identify firms that align with both ethical values and financial goals.

Blue-chip stocks serve as another essential consideration for investors focused on low-risk, high-yield opportunities. These established companies boast a track record of strong performance and reliability, making them attractive candidates for conservative investors. Metrics like dividend payout ratio and historical dividend growth rates are pivotal in assessing blue-chip stocks. A consistent ability to increase dividends over time indicates not only a robust business model but also a commitment to returning capital to shareholders, which can be particularly appealing in uncertain economic climates.

For those exploring real estate investments, REITs can offer a compelling combination of income and stability. Performance metrics specific to real estate, such as funds from operations (FFO) and net asset value (NAV), are critical in evaluating these investment trusts. By analyzing these metrics, investors can assess the intrinsic value of a REIT and its potential for generating consistent income through dividends. The volatility of the real estate market can be mitigated by focusing on REITs with strong performance metrics, making them an attractive option for income-seeking investors.

Lastly, the concept of Growth at a Reasonable Price (GARP) blends growth investing with value principles. Investors should analyze metrics that highlight both growth potential and valuation, such as PEG ratios (price/earnings to growth) and revenue growth rates. By identifying undervalued stocks poised for growth, especially in sectors like technology and renewable energy, investors can strategically position themselves for significant returns with manageable risk. Overall, a comprehensive analysis of performance metrics across various investment strategies equips investors with the tools needed to navigate the complexities of the stock market in 2025.

Recommended Blue-Chip Stocks for Investors

When considering blue-chip stocks for investment in 2025, it is essential to focus on companies that have demonstrated resilience, stability, and a commitment to shareholder returns over time. Blue-chip stocks are typically large, well-established firms with a strong market presence and a history of reliable performance. These companies are known for their ability to weather economic downturns while still providing consistent dividends, making them an attractive option for low-risk, high-yield investments. For investors seeking stability, identifying blue-chip stocks that align with current market trends and future growth prospects is crucial.

One category of blue-chip stocks worth considering is the Dividend Aristocrats. These are companies that have not only maintained but also consistently increased their dividends for at least 25 consecutive years. Investing in Dividend Aristocrats can provide a dual benefit: the potential for capital appreciation and an increasing income stream. For instance, companies in sectors such as consumer staples and utilities often fall into this category. Their stable cash flows and strong market positions allow them to return a portion of their profits to shareholders, making them ideal candidates for conservative investors looking for reliable returns.

Additionally, ESG (Environmental, Social, and Governance) investing is becoming increasingly relevant in today's market. Many blue-chip companies are now focusing on sustainable practices and corporate responsibility, which can lead to long-term performance advantages. Firms that prioritize ESG criteria tend to attract a growing base of socially conscious investors, and their commitment to sustainability can enhance their reputations and market positions. By investing in blue-chip stocks that adhere to ESG principles, investors can align their portfolios with their values while potentially mitigating risk and benefiting from solid returns.

In the realm of technology, several blue-chip companies not only lead in innovation but also pay dividends, thus providing a balanced approach to growth and income. Tech giants that have established themselves as market leaders often possess the financial strength to generate consistent cash flows, allowing them to reward shareholders with dividends. These companies are essential for investors looking to capitalize on the ongoing advancements in technology while benefiting from the stability that blue-chip stocks offer.

Lastly, for those interested in diversifying their portfolios, international blue-chip stocks can provide exposure to foreign markets known for high dividend yields with manageable risk. Investing in established companies outside of the domestic market can enhance returns and reduce volatility by spreading investments across different economic environments. By incorporating a mix of domestic and international blue-chip stocks into their portfolios, investors can achieve a balanced strategy that focuses on low-risk, high-yield opportunities while navigating the complexities of global markets in 2025.

Chapter 5: REITs (Real Estate Investment Trusts)

Understanding REIT Structures

Understanding the structure of Real Estate Investment Trusts (REITs) is essential for investors seeking consistent income and lower volatility in their portfolios. REITs are companies that own, operate, or finance income-producing real estate across a range of property sectors. They provide a way for investors to gain exposure to real estate without the direct challenges of property management. By owning shares of a REIT, individuals can participate in the rental income and capital appreciation generated by real estate, all while benefiting from the liquidity of a publicly traded stock.

There are several types of REITs, including equity, mortgage, and hybrid REITs. Equity REITs primarily invest in and manage income-producing properties, making their revenue mainly from leasing space and collecting rents. Mortgage REITs, on the other hand, provide financing for income-producing real estate by purchasing or originating mortgages and mortgage-backed securities. Hybrid REITs combine both equity and mortgage strategies, allowing for diversified income streams. This variety in structure enables investors to tailor their exposure to real estate according to their risk tolerance and income needs.

Investing in REITs can be particularly attractive for those focused on dividend income. Most REITs are required to distribute at least 90% of their taxable income to shareholders in the form of dividends to maintain their tax-advantaged status. This results in typically higher dividend yields compared to traditional stocks, making them appealing to income-focused investors, including those interested in Dividend Aristocrats. The regular income provided by REITs can help stabilize a portfolio, especially in volatile market conditions, thus aligning with defensive investment strategies.

Moreover, REITs often exhibit lower correlation with traditional equity markets, offering diversification benefits. Their performance is largely driven by the real estate market, which can be influenced by different economic factors than those affecting technology or commodity sectors. This characteristic is particularly beneficial for investors in high-risk areas such as cryptocurrencies or tech stocks, as it allows for a more balanced portfolio that can withstand market fluctuations. Investors can also consider ESG-focused REITs, which align with environmentally and socially responsible investing trends while still providing solid returns.

In conclusion, understanding REIT structures empowers investors to make informed decisions that align with their financial goals in 2025. By incorporating REITs into their investment strategy, individuals can achieve a blend of income, growth potential, and risk management. As the landscape of investment opportunities continues to evolve, REITs offer a viable option for stock market investors looking for reliable income sources and lower volatility, fitting seamlessly into broader investment themes such as GARP, sector rotation strategies, and international high-yield stocks.

Benefits of Investing in REITs

Investing in Real Estate Investment Trusts (REITs) offers numerous advantages, especially for those seeking consistent income with lower volatility. One of the primary benefits of REITs is their ability to generate regular dividend payouts. Unlike traditional stocks, which may reinvest profits for growth, REITs are mandated by law to distribute at least 90% of their taxable income as dividends to shareholders. This structure provides investors with a reliable income stream, making REITs particularly appealing for those seeking cash flow in their portfolios.

Another significant advantage of REITs is their diversification potential. Real estate often behaves differently than traditional equities and bonds, providing a hedge against market volatility. By incorporating REITs into an investment strategy, investors can reduce overall portfolio risk while still enjoying exposure to the real estate sector. This diversification is crucial for stock market investors, brokers, and those involved in various high-risk sectors, as it mitigates the impact of downturns in other asset classes.

REITs also offer liquidity, which is an essential factor for many investors. Unlike direct real estate investments that require substantial capital and come with high transaction costs, publicly traded REITs can be bought and sold on stock exchanges, providing investors with the flexibility to enter or exit positions quickly. This aspect is particularly beneficial for tech investors and those involved in fast-paced markets where rapid adjustments to portfolios are necessary.

Moreover, REITs can serve as a gateway to real estate markets that individual investors may find difficult to access. They allow investors to participate in various real estate sectors, including residential, commercial, and industrial properties, without the need for significant capital investment. This accessibility can be especially appealing to investors interested in the growth at a reasonable price (GARP) strategy, as it allows them to diversify across different real estate segments while seeking opportunities for appreciation.

Lastly, with the increasing focus on Environmental, Social, and Governance (ESG) criteria, many REITs are aligning their operations with sustainability practices. Investing in REITs that prioritize ESG factors not only supports responsible investing but also positions investors to benefit from the growing demand for sustainable real estate solutions. This alignment with socially responsible practices makes REITs an attractive option for investors looking to achieve solid returns while minimizing risk, thus enhancing their overall investment strategy in 2025.

Top Performing REITs for Consistent Income

Real Estate Investment Trusts (REITs) have emerged as a top choice for investors seeking consistent income streams while maintaining lower risk profiles. In 2025, REITs continue to attract attention due to their unique structure, which requires them to distribute at least 90% of their taxable income as dividends. This characteristic not only makes them an appealing investment for income-seeking investors, but it also positions them as a reliable option amid fluctuating market conditions. As stock market investors navigate an increasingly complex landscape, understanding the top-performing REITs can be pivotal in constructing a balanced portfolio focused on income generation.

Among the various types of REITs, those focusing on residential and commercial properties have demonstrated strong performance in recent years. For instance, multifamily housing REITs have thrived due to ongoing demand for rental units, particularly in urban areas where homeownership is less attainable for younger generations. These REITs benefit from lower vacancy rates and the ability to increase rents in a competitive housing market, translating into stable and growing dividends. Investors should consider these REITs as part of a diversified strategy, particularly as they align with the broader trend towards urbanization and changing housing needs.

Healthcare REITs also represent a compelling segment for consistent income. With an aging population and increasing demand for healthcare services, these REITs invest in properties such as hospitals, senior living facilities, and medical office buildings. Their tenants typically operate on long-term leases, offering predictable cash flow and resilience during economic downturns. This stability, coupled with the growing need for healthcare infrastructure, positions healthcare REITs as a solid choice for investors prioritizing income while managing risk.

For those focused on sustainability and social responsibility, ESG-focused REITs provide an attractive avenue. These REITs prioritize environmentally sustainable practices and social governance, appealing to investors looking to align their investment strategies with their values. Additionally, the increasing emphasis on sustainable development can enhance the long-term viability of these investments, as they cater to a growing market of environmentally conscious consumers and tenants. Investors should actively seek out ESG REITs that not only deliver solid returns but also contribute positively to societal and environmental outcomes.

Lastly, investors should pay attention to REITs involved in data centers and logistics. The rise of e-commerce and digital transformation has significantly boosted demand for data storage and distribution facilities. These REITs benefit from long-term leases and high occupancy rates, leading to consistent income streams. As technology continues to advance and online shopping habits solidify, these segments of the REIT market are likely to experience robust growth. By incorporating top-performing REITs from diverse sectors, investors can build a resilient income portfolio that thrives even in uncertain economic climates.

Chapter 6: Growth at a Reasonable Price (GARP)

GARP Investment Philosophy

The GARP investment philosophy, which stands for Growth at a Reasonable Price, is an essential strategy for investors seeking a balanced approach to stock selection. This methodology seeks to combine the principles of growth investing and value investing, allowing investors to identify stocks that are not only poised for growth but are also available at reasonable valuations. In a market characterized by volatility and uncertainty, GARP offers a pragmatic framework, appealing to a diverse range of investors, from those focused on technology and renewable energy to those interested in traditional sectors.

At the core of GARP is the recognition that growth does not have to come at any price. Investors employing this strategy look for companies that exhibit strong earnings growth potential but are trading at a price-to-earnings (P/E) ratio that is lower than their growth rates would suggest. This approach helps in mitigating risk while still capitalizing on opportunities for appreciation. For stock market investors and brokers, this means analyzing metrics such as the PEG ratio, which compares a stock's P/E ratio to its projected growth rate, making it easier to identify undervalued growth stocks.

In the context of current market dynamics, GARP can be particularly advantageous for investors in sectors such as technology and renewable energy. As innovation drives growth in these fields, identifying companies that are not only leaders in their industries but are also trading at attractive valuations can yield substantial returns. For example, tech firms that consistently innovate while maintaining stable earnings can be prime GARP candidates, providing the dual benefit of growth and income through dividends. This strategy aligns well with the interests of tech investors looking for sustainable opportunities amid rapid market changes.

Moreover, GARP investing seamlessly integrates with other investment strategies, such as ESG investing and blue-chip stock selection. By focusing on companies that demonstrate both growth potential and responsible business practices, GARP investors can align their portfolios with ethical considerations while still aiming for solid financial returns. This dual focus on societal impact and profitability appeals to a growing segment of investors who prioritize sustainability alongside financial success.

In conclusion, GARP investment philosophy serves as a strategic framework for navigating the complexities of the stock market in 2025. By combining growth and value principles, this approach allows investors to uncover opportunities in both traditional and emerging sectors, from real estate investment trusts to defensive stocks. As market conditions evolve, incorporating GARP into investment strategies can enhance the potential for high yields while managing risk, making it an invaluable tool for both seasoned and new investors alike.

Identifying GARP Opportunities

Identifying GARP opportunities involves a strategic blend of growth and value investing principles, targeting stocks that are not only undervalued but also exhibit strong growth potential. Investors seeking to implement GARP strategies should focus on companies that demonstrate a consistent history of earnings growth, paired with reasonable price-to-earnings ratios. This dual focus allows investors to capitalize on the upside of growth while maintaining a cushion against market volatility, making GARP an appealing strategy for those looking to balance risk and reward.

To effectively identify GARP opportunities, investors should start by analyzing a company's fundamentals. Key metrics to consider include earnings per share growth, return on equity, and debt levels. Companies with a solid track record of increasing earnings and manageable debt are often better positioned to sustain growth. Additionally, assessing the price-to-earnings growth (PEG) ratio can provide insight into whether a stock is reasonably priced relative to its expected growth rate. A lower PEG ratio often signals a potential GARP opportunity, indicating that the stock may be undervalued compared to its growth prospects.

Another important aspect of identifying GARP stocks is to examine the broader market trends and sector performance. Sectors that are poised for growth, such as technology, renewable energy, and healthcare, often harbor companies that fit the GARP profile. Investors should pay attention to macroeconomic indicators and industry-specific developments that could influence growth rates. By focusing on sectors with strong growth potential while maintaining a value-oriented approach, investors can increase their chances of discovering lucrative GARP opportunities.

Furthermore, it is essential to consider qualitative factors that may impact a company's growth trajectory. These include competitive advantages, management effectiveness, and market positioning. Companies that possess unique value propositions or strong brand loyalty are more likely to sustain growth over time. Investors should conduct thorough research on these qualitative aspects alongside quantitative analysis to build a comprehensive view of potential GARP candidates.

Lastly, diversifying investments across various GARP opportunities can mitigate risks associated with individual stocks. Investors should consider building a diversified portfolio that includes a mix of GARP stocks from different sectors and geographies. This approach not only reduces exposure to sector-specific downturns but also enhances the potential for capturing growth across various market conditions. By systematically applying these principles, investors can effectively identify GARP opportunities that align with their investment goals in the dynamic landscape of 2025.

Successful GARP Strategies for 2025

Successful GARP (Growth at a Reasonable Price) strategies for 2025 emphasize identifying stocks that combine strong growth prospects with attractive valuations. Investors should focus on companies exhibiting robust earnings growth without trading at excessive price-to-earnings ratios. This approach is particularly effective in a dynamic market environment where growth stocks can be overvalued, and finding those that remain reasonably priced allows for capturing upside potential while mitigating risk. GARP investors should leverage a mix of fundamental analysis and market sentiment to uncover opportunities that can yield significant returns.

Dividend Aristocrats stand out as prime candidates for GARP strategies in 2025. These companies have a proven track record of increasing dividends over long periods, showcasing their financial stability and commitment to returning value to shareholders. By investing in Dividend Aristocrats, investors can achieve a steady income stream while benefiting from potential price appreciation. The focus should be on firms that not only maintain dividend growth but also exhibit resilience in their business models, making them suitable for a GARP approach.

ESG (Environmental, Social, and Governance) investing is another pivotal area in which GARP strategies can thrive. As investors increasingly prioritize sustainability, companies that adhere to ESG principles are likely to see enhanced performance and lower risk profiles. GARP investors should seek out firms that balance growth with responsibility, as these companies are often better positioned to handle regulatory challenges and changing consumer preferences. By integrating ESG factors into stock selection, investors can identify undervalued stocks poised for growth while aligning with broader societal goals.

Incorporating technology dividends into GARP strategies presents a unique opportunity for investors looking to blend growth with income. Many technology companies are not only at the forefront of innovation but also provide dividends, allowing investors to benefit from both capital appreciation and regular income. Identifying tech firms that offer reasonable valuations in relation to their growth prospects can lead to lucrative investments. As technology continues to evolve, focusing on companies with sustainable competitive advantages will be crucial in discerning long-term winners.

Lastly, implementing sector rotation strategies is essential for GARP investors, particularly in an economic climate characterized by volatility. By understanding economic cycles and adjusting allocations to sectors that perform well at different stages, investors can enhance their portfolios' resilience. Key sectors to watch include utilities and consumer staples during downturns, while growth sectors like technology and healthcare may offer opportunities during expansions. A well-executed sector rotation strategy can help GARP investors capitalize on market trends while maintaining a balanced risk profile.

Chapter 7: Defensive Stocks

Characteristics of Defensive Stocks

Defensive stocks are characterized by their ability to provide stability and consistent returns, especially during periods of economic uncertainty. These stocks typically belong to sectors that produce essential goods and services, such as utilities, consumer staples, and healthcare. Investors often turn to these sectors when the market faces downturns, as the demand for their products tends to remain relatively constant regardless of economic conditions. This inherent stability makes defensive stocks an attractive choice for those seeking lower-risk investment options.

One of the defining features of defensive stocks is their resilience in the face of economic fluctuations. Companies in these sectors often possess strong balance sheets, allowing them to weather downturns better than their more cyclical counterparts. For instance, utility companies deliver essential services that consumers rely on, regardless of economic circumstances. Similarly, consumer staples, such as food and household products, experience steady demand, which helps buffer these companies against economic shocks. This stability is a significant draw for investors looking to mitigate risk in their portfolios.

Another characteristic of defensive stocks is their tendency to pay dividends consistently. Many of these companies have a history of not only maintaining but also increasing their dividends over time. This makes defensive stocks particularly appealing to income-focused investors who prioritize steady cash flow. Dividend Aristocrats, for example, are a group of companies known for their long-standing practice of increasing dividends annually, which underscores their financial health and commitment to returning value to shareholders.

Moreover, defensive stocks often provide a hedge against market volatility. By incorporating these stocks into a diversified portfolio, investors can reduce overall risk while still achieving reasonable returns. This strategy is particularly beneficial for those who may be heavily invested in more volatile sectors, such as technology or cryptocurrencies. By balancing high-risk investments with stable, defensive stocks, investors can create a more resilient investment strategy that can better withstand market fluctuations.

Lastly, the appeal of defensive stocks is heightened by their potential role in ESG investing. Many investors are increasingly focused on environmental and social responsibility, and several defensive sectors align well with these values. Companies that prioritize sustainable practices while delivering essential services can appeal to socially conscious investors. This intersection of stability and responsibility makes defensive stocks an essential consideration for investors looking to build a low-risk, high-yield portfolio in 2025 and beyond.

Sectors to Focus On

Investors looking for opportunities in 2025 should consider sectors that not only promise growth but also offer stability and lower risk. One such sector is Dividend Aristocrats, which includes companies with a strong history of increasing dividends consistently. These companies demonstrate financial health and resilience, making them attractive for investors seeking reliable income. As economic uncertainties persist, focusing on firms that have a long-standing commitment to returning value to shareholders can provide a buffer against market volatility.

Another critical area to explore is ESG investing, which emphasizes environmentally and socially responsible companies. As consumers and investors increasingly prioritize sustainability, businesses that adhere to ESG principles are likely to thrive in the long run. These companies often enjoy stronger brand loyalty and reduced regulatory risks, making them appealing for those seeking solid returns with lower risk profiles. Additionally, investing in ESG-focused firms aligns financial goals with ethical considerations, a growing priority for many investors.

Blue-chip stocks represent another reliable investment avenue. These established companies are known for their stability, reliability, and solid performance over time. Investing in blue-chip stocks can be particularly advantageous during economic downturns, as these companies typically possess strong balance sheets and competitive advantages. They also often distribute dividends, providing investors with both growth potential and income, thus appealing to a wide range of investors from conservative to growth-oriented.

Real Estate Investment Trusts (REITs) offer another compelling option for those seeking consistent income with lower volatility. By investing in REITs, investors can gain exposure to the real estate market without the complexities of direct property ownership. REITs typically provide high dividend yields and can serve as a hedge against inflation, making them a strategic addition to any diversified portfolio. Furthermore, they offer liquidity and the potential for capital appreciation, appealing to both income-focused and growth-oriented investors.

Lastly, investors should not overlook the potential of low-volatility ETFs. These exchange-traded funds concentrate on stocks that exhibit lower price fluctuations, providing a smoother investment experience during turbulent market conditions. By carefully selecting sectors that perform well in various economic cycles, such as defensive sectors or technology dividends, investors can mitigate risks while still targeting growth. Incorporating these strategies into an investment portfolio can help enhance returns while preserving capital, aligning perfectly with the goals of savvy investors in 2025.

Analyzing Performance During Economic Downturns

Economic downturns present unique challenges and opportunities for investors. During these periods, stock performance is often volatile, making it essential to analyze how different sectors and asset classes react under stress. Investors seeking low-risk, high-yield stocks must consider historical performance trends, economic indicators, and the resilience of specific industries. Assessing how previous downturns affected various investments can provide valuable insights for strategizing in 2025.

Dividend Aristocrats are one category of stocks that have historically weathered economic storms effectively. These companies have a proven track record of increasing dividends year after year, which speaks to their financial stability and commitment to returning value to shareholders. By focusing on these long-standing firms, investors can identify opportunities that not only offer steady income but are also likely to maintain performance during recessions. This stability is particularly appealing to investors prioritizing low-risk strategies in uncertain economic climates.

Another strategy to consider is ESG investing, which focuses on companies that are environmentally and socially responsible. Research has shown that firms with strong ESG practices tend to exhibit lower volatility and better risk-adjusted returns, making them attractive during economic downturns. By prioritizing investments in sustainable businesses, investors can align their portfolios with responsible practices while potentially enhancing their financial performance. This dual benefit makes ESG stocks a compelling choice for those looking to mitigate risk.

Blue-chip stocks also play a crucial role in a low-risk investment strategy during economic downturns. These established companies offer a history of reliability and strong performance, often maintaining dividends even in challenging economic conditions. Investing in blue-chip stocks can provide a cushion against market volatility while ensuring that investors have exposure to companies with strong fundamentals. This strategy aligns well with the goal of achieving high yield with manageable risk.

Moreover, defensive stocks and sectors, such as utilities and consumer staples, tend to remain stable when economic conditions worsen. These sectors provide essential goods and services, making them less susceptible to economic fluctuations. By incorporating defensive stocks into a diversified investment portfolio, investors can protect themselves against downturns while still pursuing growth opportunities. This balanced approach is vital for those looking to navigate the complexities of the stock market effectively in 2025.

Chapter 8: International High-Yield Stocks

Benefits of International Diversification

International diversification offers a range of benefits for stock market investors seeking to enhance their portfolios in 2025. By spreading investments across different countries and regions, investors can significantly reduce the risk associated with domestic market fluctuations. This strategy allows for the capture of growth opportunities in emerging markets while also taking advantage of stable economies. As market conditions can vary greatly from one country to another, international diversification helps mitigate the impact of localized economic downturns, providing a buffer against volatility.

One of the primary advantages of investing internationally lies in the potential for higher dividend yields. Many foreign markets, particularly in developing economies, offer attractive dividend-paying stocks that may not be available domestically. This can be especially appealing for those focused on income generation through Dividend Aristocrats or International High-Yield Stocks. By investing in these markets, investors can tap into companies that have a history of stable and increasing dividends, enhancing their overall income potential while managing risk.

Moreover, international investments can provide exposure to sectors and industries that may be underrepresented in the domestic market. For instance, investors interested in tech, EV vehicles, or renewable energy may find promising opportunities in foreign companies that are leading in these sectors. This allows for a more comprehensive approach to growth at a reasonable price (GARP) as investors can identify undervalued stocks poised for significant growth internationally. Additionally, sectors like utilities and consumer staples, often regarded as defensive stocks, can offer stability in uncertain times, further balancing the portfolio.

Geopolitical diversification is another essential aspect of reducing risk. By investing in various regions, investors can shield themselves from political instability or regulatory changes that may adversely affect their domestic holdings. This is particularly relevant for those investing in sectors like oil, fossil fuels, or emerging technologies like AI and space exploration, where government policies can have significant impacts. A diversified international portfolio can thus serve as a safeguard against such uncertainties, ensuring more consistent performance across different environments.

Lastly, international diversification aligns well with the principles of ESG investing. Many foreign companies are at the forefront of sustainable practices and social responsibility, offering investors an opportunity to engage in ethical investing while still pursuing solid returns. By integrating these considerations into their investment strategy, investors can benefit from the potential for lower risk in addition to aligning their portfolios with their values. In conclusion, the benefits of international diversification in 2025 are manifold, providing stock market investors with a strategic approach to achieving low-risk, high-yield outcomes.

Identifying High-Yield Opportunities Abroad

Identifying high-yield opportunities abroad requires a strategic approach that balances potential returns with manageable risk. Investors should begin by analyzing international markets that demonstrate stable economic conditions and favorable regulatory environments. Countries with established financial systems, such as Germany, Canada, and Australia, often provide a fertile ground for high-yield investments. By focusing on these regions, investors can tap into local companies with strong performance histories, particularly those that have consistently offered attractive dividends. Conducting thorough research on foreign exchange risks and political stability further enhances decision-making in this context.

One effective strategy for finding high-yield stocks abroad is to look for Dividend Aristocrats in international markets. These are companies with a proven track record of increasing dividends over a significant period, typically 25 years or more. By identifying such firms, investors can rest assured that their investments are in stable entities that prioritize shareholder returns. For instance, many European companies have established themselves as Dividend Aristocrats, offering reliable income streams alongside the potential for capital appreciation. This approach not only provides a cushion during volatile market conditions but also aligns with a long-term investment strategy focused on income generation.

In addition to Dividend Aristocrats, ESG (Environmental, Social, and Governance) investing has gained traction as a viable option for those looking to diversify internationally. By focusing on companies that prioritize sustainability and ethical practices, investors can align their portfolios with their values while still seeking solid returns. Many international firms are increasingly adopting ESG principles, which can lead to improved operational efficiencies and reduced risks over time. Investing in these companies often results in lower volatility and appealing yields, making them suitable for risk-averse investors seeking high-paying stocks.

Another category to consider is international Blue-Chip stocks, which represent established companies in foreign markets with strong performance records. These firms often operate in sectors with high barriers to entry, ensuring stability even during economic downturns. By investing in Blue-Chip stocks abroad, investors can gain exposure to global economic growth while benefiting from the companies' robust financial health. This strategy can also be complemented by sector rotation tactics that allow investors to adjust their portfolios based on economic cycles, maximizing returns from sectors that are likely to perform well at any given time.

Lastly, Real Estate Investment Trusts (REITs) and low-volatility exchange-traded funds (ETFs) focused on international markets can provide additional avenues for income generation with reduced risk. REITs offer exposure to real estate investments abroad, often yielding attractive dividends while diversifying away from traditional equities. Similarly, low-volatility ETFs that concentrate on international stocks can help investors capitalize on stable, high-yield opportunities without facing the full brunt of market fluctuations. By implementing these strategies, investors can effectively identify and leverage high-yield opportunities in the global arena while maintaining a low-risk profile.

Managing Currency and Political Risks

In today's interconnected global economy, managing currency and political risks is essential for stock market investors aiming to maximize returns while minimizing potential losses. Currency fluctuations can significantly impact the profitability of investments, particularly for those venturing into international markets. For instance, when investing in foreign stocks or real estate investment trusts (REITs), the value of dividends or rental income can be adversely affected by changes in currency exchange rates. Investors should consider diversifying their portfolios with assets that are less sensitive to currency variations, or utilize hedging strategies to protect against unfavorable movements.

Political risks, including changes in government policies, regulatory environments, and geopolitical tensions, can also pose significant threats to investment returns. For example, companies operating in sectors such as oil and gas or technology may face regulatory changes that impact their profitability. Investors should conduct thorough research on the political climate of countries where they are investing, looking for indicators of stability or potential volatility. Engaging with resources that provide insights into political risk assessments can help investors make informed decisions about where to allocate their capital.

Additionally, focusing on companies with a strong history of resilience during political turbulence can be a smart strategy. Dividend Aristocrats, which are companies with a track record of consistent dividend growth, often weather economic downturns more effectively than their peers. These companies typically possess solid fundamentals and strong market positions, allowing them to maintain their dividend payments even in challenging environments. This stability can provide a cushion against both currency and political risks, making them an attractive option for low-risk, high-yield investment strategies.

Environmental, social, and governance (ESG) investing is another approach to mitigating risks associated with currency and politics. Companies that prioritize sustainable practices and social responsibility tend to attract a loyal consumer base and face fewer regulatory hurdles. By investing in ESG-compliant firms, investors not only align their portfolios with their values but also reduce their exposure to risks related to environmental legislation and social unrest. This strategy is particularly relevant in the current landscape, where issues such as climate change and social equity are increasingly influencing market dynamics.

Finally, investors should remain vigilant and adaptive, employing sector rotation strategies to navigate changing economic conditions. By reallocating investments based on the performance of various sectors, investors can capitalize on opportunities while minimizing exposure to risks. Low-volatility exchange-traded funds (ETFs) can also serve as a practical tool for achieving this goal, providing a diversified approach to investing in stocks that exhibit lower price fluctuations. Through careful management of currency and political risks, investors can enhance their chances of achieving stable, high-yield returns in the evolving market landscape of 2025.

Chapter 9: Technology Dividends

The Rise of Dividend-Paying Tech Stocks

The landscape of technology investing has undergone a significant transformation in recent years, with a notable rise in dividend-paying tech stocks. Traditionally, the tech sector has been characterized by rapid growth and reinvestment of profits into innovation rather than returning capital to shareholders. However, as the market matures, an increasing number of tech companies are adopting dividend policies, signaling a shift towards a more balanced approach that combines growth with income. This trend is particularly appealing to investors seeking low-risk, high-yield opportunities in an ever-evolving market.

Dividend Aristocrats within the tech sector are companies that have consistently increased their dividends over time while maintaining operational stability. These firms not only showcase strong fundamentals but also emphasize long-term value creation for their shareholders. Investors focusing on these tech Dividend Aristocrats can benefit from both the potential for capital appreciation and a reliable income stream, making them an attractive option for those looking to mitigate risk while pursuing growth. Notable examples include established players that have embraced dividend payouts, indicating a commitment to returning value to their investors.

ESG investing has also started to influence the rise of dividend-paying tech stocks. Companies that prioritize environmental and social governance are increasingly recognized for their sustainable business practices, which can contribute to lower risk profiles. By investing in tech companies that align with ESG principles, investors can access a dual benefit: solid returns coupled with responsible investing. This trend is particularly relevant as more investors seek to align their portfolios with their values, ensuring that their investments contribute to a positive impact while still providing the financial benefits associated with dividends.

Blue-chip stocks in the technology sector are becoming increasingly attractive as they combine reliability with growth potential. These established firms have demonstrated resilience across economic cycles, making them a sound choice for conservative investors. The stability of blue-chip tech companies, coupled with a commitment to returning dividends, positions them well within a diversified investment strategy. As the market continues to evolve, these stocks offer a safety net for investors while still allowing them to participate in the growth opportunities that the tech sector presents.

Finally, the integration of Growth at a Reasonable Price (GARP) strategies into the tech investment landscape emphasizes the pursuit of undervalued stocks that are poised for growth. This approach encourages investors to identify tech companies that not only have strong growth potential but also provide dividends, effectively balancing risk and reward. By focusing on these stocks, investors can capitalize on the growth of the tech industry while enjoying the income that dividends provide. This combination of strategies positions dividend-paying tech stocks as a compelling choice for investors seeking to navigate the complexities of the stock market in 2025.

Evaluating Tech Companies with Strong Dividends

Evaluating tech companies with strong dividends involves a multifaceted approach that balances potential growth with the reliability of income. In the realm of technology, many investors traditionally focus on capital appreciation, often overlooking the substantial benefits of dividend-paying tech stocks. Companies like Apple, Microsoft, and Intel not only lead the market in innovation but also have established themselves as reliable sources of income through consistent dividend payments. This dual focus on growth and income makes them particularly appealing to investors seeking low-risk, high-yield opportunities in 2025.

To effectively evaluate these companies, investors should first consider their dividend history. Dividend Aristocrats are firms that have consistently increased their dividends for at least 25 years. These companies exemplify stability, making them an attractive choice for those looking to mitigate risk while still benefiting from the growth potential inherent in the tech sector. Analyzing their payout ratios, which indicate the proportion of earnings paid out as dividends, can provide insights into their financial health and sustainability of dividend payments. A lower payout ratio often suggests that the company has room to grow both its business and its dividends.

ESG (Environmental, Social, and Governance) factors are increasingly important for investors who wish to align their portfolios with socially responsible practices while still seeking strong returns. Many tech companies are making strides in sustainability, which not only enhances their corporate reputation but can also lead to improved financial performance. By focusing on companies that prioritize ESG principles, investors can find tech stocks that not only offer dividends but also contribute positively to societal goals, thus reducing long-term risks associated with regulatory changes and shifting consumer preferences.

In addition to traditional dividend-paying tech stocks, investors should also consider the potential of Real Estate Investment Trusts (REITs) that focus on technology-driven properties or data centers. These investments can provide consistent income streams while benefiting from the growing demand for tech infrastructure. Moreover, exploring international high-yield stocks can diversify portfolios, offering exposure to tech companies in emerging markets that may provide higher dividend yields with manageable risks. This approach can enhance overall returns and reduce volatility by spreading investments across different geographical regions.

Lastly, employing a Growth at a Reasonable Price (GARP) strategy can assist investors in identifying undervalued tech stocks poised for growth while also providing dividends. By analyzing companies that exhibit strong growth potential yet remain reasonably priced, investors can position themselves advantageously in a competitive market. Additionally, incorporating low-volatility ETFs that focus on dividend-paying tech stocks can provide an extra layer of security, enabling investors to benefit from steady returns while minimizing exposure to market fluctuations. In this way, evaluating tech companies with strong dividends becomes a strategic endeavor that balances risk and reward effectively.

Future Trends in Technology Dividends

Future trends in technology dividends are set to reshape the investment landscape, particularly for stock market investors looking for reliable income streams. As the technology sector continues to evolve, companies are increasingly recognizing the importance of returning value to shareholders through dividends. This shift is driven by the need for stability and investor confidence in an era marked by rapid innovation and market volatility. Tech companies that consistently pay dividends are likely to attract a broader base of investors, especially those focused on balancing growth with income.

One significant trend is the emergence of dividend-paying tech firms that have traditionally reinvested profits into growth initiatives. As these companies mature, many are shifting their strategies to include regular dividend payments, reflecting a commitment to shareholder value. Investors should pay particular attention to "Dividend Aristocrats" within the tech sector—companies with a proven history of increasing dividends over time. These firms often demonstrate resilience and stability, making them attractive options for those seeking low-risk, high-yield investments.

Another noteworthy development is the integration of Environmental, Social, and Governance (ESG) factors into investment strategies. As more investors prioritize sustainability, tech companies that adhere to ESG principles are likely to see increased demand for their stocks. This trend not only supports social responsibility but also aligns with the pursuit of solid returns with reduced risk. Firms that successfully balance innovation with ethical practices are poised to offer dividends that attract socially conscious investors while maintaining financial performance.

In addition, the rise of blue-chip stocks within the technology sector presents an opportunity for investors seeking reliability and strong performance. These established companies often have robust financial health, making them well-positioned to weather economic downturns while continuing to distribute dividends. Investors should focus on identifying blue-chip tech stocks that have consistently demonstrated their ability to generate cash flow and maintain shareholder returns, thus providing a stable income source amidst market fluctuations.

Lastly, the growth at a reasonable price (GARP) strategy is gaining traction among tech investors. By identifying undervalued technology stocks poised for growth, investors can capitalize on price appreciation while also benefiting from dividend yields. This approach allows investors to navigate the dynamic tech landscape effectively, seeking out companies that are not only innovative but also financially sound enough to reward shareholders consistently. As the technology sector continues to mature, those who adopt a strategic focus on dividends will likely find themselves well-positioned for success in the evolving market of 2025.

Chapter 10: Sector Rotation Strategies

Understanding Economic Cycles

Economic cycles are fundamental to understanding the stock market's behavior and can significantly influence investment strategies. These cycles, characterized by periods of expansion and contraction, affect various sectors differently. Investors and brokers must recognize the distinct phases of these cycles—expansion, peak, contraction, and trough—to align their investment strategies accordingly. For instance, during expansions, cyclical sectors like technology and consumer discretionary often thrive, while defensive sectors such as utilities and consumer staples provide stability during downturns. By identifying where the economy stands within this cycle, investors can make informed decisions about their portfolio allocations.

The concept of sector rotation is crucial for navigating economic cycles effectively. Different sectors respond uniquely to the shifting economic landscape, meaning that investments should be adjusted as the cycle progresses. For example, during economic growth, investors might lean toward growth stocks, particularly in technology and emerging industries like electric vehicles and AI. Conversely, in periods of contraction, defensive stocks and dividend-paying blue-chip companies become more attractive due to their stability and reliable income streams. Understanding which sectors are likely to perform well at any given stage of the cycle can enhance the potential for higher yields while managing risk.

Investors should also consider the impact of macroeconomic indicators, such as interest rates, inflation, and employment data, which can signal changes in economic cycles. For instance, rising interest rates may indicate a peak or contraction phase, prompting a shift towards low-volatility ETFs or REITs that provide steady income. Keeping abreast of these indicators allows investors to anticipate market shifts and adjust their strategies proactively, minimizing exposure to sectors that may underperform and capitalizing on opportunities in those that are poised for growth.

In the context of current trends, ESG investing has gained traction during these cycles, as investors increasingly prioritize sustainable practices. Companies that adhere to environmental and social governance principles tend to exhibit resilience during economic downturns, making them appealing for low-risk investments. Furthermore, technology companies that combine innovation with dividends offer a balanced approach, allowing investors to benefit from growth while enjoying the stability of income. This dual focus can be particularly advantageous in fluctuating economic conditions.

Ultimately, understanding economic cycles equips investors with the knowledge to identify the best strategies for investing in high-paying, low-risk stocks in 2025. By recognizing the phases of the cycle, employing sector rotation strategies, and being mindful of macroeconomic indicators, investors can enhance their portfolios with a mix of Dividend Aristocrats, blue-chip stocks, and international high-yield opportunities. This informed approach not only aims for solid returns but also helps mitigate risk, aligning with the overarching goal of achieving financial growth in a dynamic economic landscape.

Key Sectors to Rotate Through in 2025

In 2025, stock market investors should consider rotating through key sectors that are poised for growth while maintaining lower risk. One of the most promising sectors is technology, particularly companies that blend innovation with dividend payouts. As the tech landscape evolves, firms that provide consistent dividends alongside cutting-edge advancements offer a balanced approach for investors seeking both income and growth potential. This sector includes established players with a track record of reliability, making them attractive for those adhering to a strategy focused on Dividend Aristocrats.

Another sector to watch is real estate, specifically through Real Estate Investment Trusts (REITs). REITs have historically provided consistent income with lower volatility compared to traditional stocks. With interest rates stabilizing and housing demand remaining robust, REITs can deliver attractive yields while diversifying an investment portfolio. Investors should focus on REITs that prioritize sustainable practices and have a history of weathering economic fluctuations, aligning with the growing trend of ESG investing.

The energy sector also presents opportunities, particularly in renewable energy and electric vehicle (EV) technologies. As the global economy shifts towards sustainable solutions, companies involved in EV batteries and infrastructure are likely to see significant growth. Investors looking for lower-risk options can target established firms with a history of profitability and a commitment to innovation. This sector aligns well with a GARP strategy, allowing investors to capitalize on undervalued stocks positioned for future expansion.

Defensive stocks, particularly in utilities and consumer staples, will remain critical in 2025, especially during economic downturns. These sectors typically show resilience in volatile markets, offering steady returns and lower risk. Investors should consider including these stocks in their portfolios to provide stability and consistent dividends, ensuring a balanced approach to investment during uncertain times.

Lastly, international high-yield stocks present a compelling opportunity for diversification. By exploring foreign markets that offer high dividend yields with manageable risk, investors can enhance their portfolios while mitigating exposure to domestic market fluctuations. This strategy complements sector rotation approaches, enabling investors to capitalize on global economic trends while enjoying the benefits of steady income streams. As 2025 unfolds, a strategic focus on these key sectors will be essential for navigating the investment landscape effectively.

Implementing a Sector Rotation Strategy

Implementing a sector rotation strategy involves strategically reallocating investments among various sectors of the economy based on their performance relative to economic cycles. This approach allows investors to capitalize on cyclical trends, optimizing returns while seeking to minimize risks. By understanding the economic indicators that signal shifts in market conditions, investors can identify which sectors are poised for growth and which may be headed for a downturn. The goal is to enhance portfolio performance by investing in sectors that are expected to outperform during specific phases of the economic cycle.

To effectively implement a sector rotation strategy, it is crucial to analyze economic indicators such as GDP growth, unemployment rates, inflation, and consumer spending. These indicators provide insight into the overall economic environment and help predict which sectors will thrive in the current conditions. For instance, during periods of economic expansion, sectors like technology and consumer discretionary often perform well, while defensive sectors such as utilities may lag. Conversely, in times of economic downturn, defensive stocks tend to maintain stability, making them more attractive to risk-averse investors.

An essential component of a successful sector rotation strategy is the timely execution of trades. Investors should remain vigilant and ready to adjust their portfolios based on emerging economic trends.

This requires continuous monitoring of market conditions and a willingness to pivot quickly when necessary. Utilizing tools such as economic calendars, financial news, and sector performance analyses can empower investors to make informed decisions and capitalize on short-term opportunities while avoiding potential pitfalls.

Investors can also consider integrating Exchange-Traded Funds (ETFs) that focus on specific sectors within their rotation strategy. Low-volatility ETFs can offer a way to gain exposure to sectors with less price fluctuation, which is particularly useful during uncertain economic times. By choosing sector-specific ETFs, investors can easily shift their allocations without the complexities of buying and selling individual stocks, making sector rotation more accessible and efficient.

In conclusion, implementing a sector rotation strategy requires a comprehensive understanding of economic cycles, timely execution, and the flexibility to adjust portfolios as conditions change. By focusing on sectors likely to outperform based on economic indicators, investors can enhance their potential for high yields while managing risk. This approach not only aligns with the pursuit of low-risk, high-yield investments but also complements various investment strategies, including ESG investing, dividend growth, and blue-chip stock strategies, ultimately leading to a more resilient and profitable portfolio.

Chapter 11: Low-Volatility ETFs

Benefits of Low-Volatility Investments

Low-volatility investments present a compelling opportunity for investors seeking stability and consistent returns in a fluctuating market. One primary benefit is the reduction in risk associated with these investments. Stocks that exhibit lower volatility tend to be less susceptible to market swings, making them an attractive option for those looking to preserve capital while still participating in equity markets. This characteristic is particularly appealing during periods of economic uncertainty, where market sentiment can lead to dramatic price fluctuations. By focusing on low-volatility stocks, investors can safeguard their portfolios against extreme downturns, potentially leading to more predictable performance over time.

Additionally, low-volatility investments often provide solid dividend yields, which can enhance total returns. Many companies categorized as low-volatility, such as Dividend Aristocrats and established blue-chip stocks, have a history of not only maintaining but also increasing their dividend payouts. This steady income can be especially beneficial for income-focused investors or those relying on dividends for cash flow.

The combination of regular dividend payments with capital appreciation creates a balanced investment approach, allowing investors to enjoy the benefits of both income and growth without exposing themselves to excessive risk.

Moreover, low-volatility stocks frequently belong to sectors that demonstrate resilience during economic downturns. Defensive stocks, such as those in utilities and consumer staples, tend to perform consistently regardless of market conditions. This stability can be advantageous for investors looking to navigate through economic cycles while minimizing exposure to more volatile sectors. By strategically allocating investments into these more stable areas, investors can maintain a robust portfolio that can weather various economic climates, making low-volatility investments a cornerstone of a long-term investment strategy.

The rise of ESG (Environmental, Social, and Governance) investing further enhances the appeal of low-volatility investments. Companies that prioritize sustainability and social responsibility often experience lower volatility due to their stable business models and strong brand loyalty. Investors increasingly seek to align their portfolios with their values, and low-volatility ESG stocks offer the dual benefit of ethical investing while still providing a potential for steady returns. This growing trend indicates that low-volatility investments can also fulfill personal and societal goals, making them a more attractive choice for a broader audience of investors.

Finally, utilizing low-volatility ETFs can streamline the investment process and provide diversification benefits. These exchange-traded funds focus on companies with lower price fluctuations, allowing investors to gain exposure to a basket of low-volatility stocks without the need for extensive individual stock analysis. This can be particularly advantageous for investors in niche markets, such as tech or international high-yield stocks, who may seek to balance their portfolios with lower-risk options. By incorporating low-volatility ETFs into their investment strategies, investors can achieve a more stable performance while still pursuing high-yield opportunities in a diversified manner.

Top Low-Volatility ETFs to Consider

Low-volatility exchange-traded funds (ETFs) have gained significant traction among investors seeking stability and consistent returns in an unpredictable market. These funds typically invest in stocks that exhibit lower price fluctuations, making them an attractive option for those looking to minimize risk while still participating in equity markets. Investors are increasingly interested in low-volatility ETFs as they align well with strategies focused on income generation and capital preservation, especially in a landscape marked by economic uncertainty.

One of the top low-volatility ETFs to consider is the Invesco S&P 500 Low Volatility ETF (SPLV). This fund includes stocks from the S&P 500 that have historically exhibited the least price volatility. By concentrating on defensive sectors such as utilities and consumer staples, SPLV has shown resilience during market downturns. Its diversified approach allows investors to benefit from stable earnings and dividends, catering to those interested in long-standing, reliable companies.

Another noteworthy option is the iShares Edge MSCI Minimum Volatility USA ETF (USMV). This ETF targets U.S. stocks with lower volatility characteristics, providing exposure to a broad range of sectors and industries. USMV has become a favorite among risk-averse investors because it seeks to deliver returns similar to those of the broader market while minimizing downside risk. The fund's focus on quality companies with strong fundamentals makes it appealing for those looking to balance growth potential with stability.

For international exposure, the Invesco S&P International Developed Low Volatility ETF (IDLV) delivers a diversified mix of low-volatility stocks from developed markets outside the U.S. This ETF is particularly relevant for investors seeking to diversify their portfolios while maintaining a focus on lower risk. By targeting global companies with stable earnings and solid dividend histories,

IDLV allows investors to tap into international markets without the heightened volatility often associated with foreign investments.

Finally, the iShares Edge MSCI Minimum Volatility Global ETF (ACWV) offers a unique global perspective by investing in low-volatility stocks from both developed and emerging markets. This ETF can be an excellent choice for investors looking to diversify their holdings across different geographic regions while still prioritizing stability. By focusing on companies with lower price fluctuations, ACWV provides an opportunity to achieve steady returns in a variety of economic conditions, aligning well with the broader investment strategies discussed in this book.

Strategies for Incorporating ETFs in Your Portfolio

Incorporating ETFs into your investment portfolio can be an effective strategy for achieving a balanced approach to low-risk, high-yield stocks. ETFs, or exchange-traded funds, offer diversification, liquidity, and typically lower fees compared to mutual funds. By strategically selecting ETFs that align with your investment goals, you can gain exposure to various sectors, including technology, real estate, and international markets, while maintaining a focus on long-term growth and stability. This is particularly relevant for investors interested in sectors such as EVs, technology, and ESG-focused companies.

One effective strategy is to target low-volatility ETFs, which consist of stocks that exhibit less price fluctuation. These funds are particularly attractive for risk-averse investors who seek steady returns amidst market volatility. By incorporating low-volatility ETFs that track defensive sectors like utilities and consumer staples, you can mitigate risk while benefiting from potential dividends. This approach not only provides a buffer during economic downturns but also allows for consistent income generation, appealing to those focused on high-yield investments.

Another strategy to consider is sector rotation through ETFs. This involves reallocating your investments based on the economic cycle to capitalize on sectors expected to perform well. For instance, during an economic expansion, technology and consumer discretionary sectors may outperform, while defensive sectors may do better during downturns. By utilizing sector-focused ETFs, you can adjust your exposure in real-time, ensuring that your portfolio remains aligned with prevailing market conditions and economic indicators, ultimately enhancing your risk-adjusted returns.

Investors can also leverage ETFs that focus on international high-yield stocks. Global diversification is essential for reducing risk and enhancing potential returns, especially in a landscape where certain foreign markets may offer attractive yields with manageable risk. By investing in ETFs that concentrate on dividend-paying companies from emerging markets, you can tap into growth opportunities outside your domestic market, further broadening your investment horizons.

Lastly, integrating ESG-focused ETFs into your portfolio can align your investment strategy with socially responsible principles while still targeting solid returns. These ETFs invest in companies that prioritize environmental and social governance, which can lead to lower risk profiles and appealing long-term performance. As consumer and regulatory pressures increase for sustainable practices, companies that prioritize ESG factors may not only provide stability but also potential growth, making them an essential component of a well-rounded investment strategy for 2025 and beyond.

Chapter 12: Conclusion

Recap of Smart Investment Strategies

Recapping smart investment strategies is essential for stock market investors seeking to navigate the complexities of the financial landscape in 2025. One of the most reliable methods remains the identification of Dividend Aristocrats. These are companies that have consistently increased their dividends over an extended period, demonstrating both financial stability and a commitment to returning value to shareholders. By focusing on these established firms, investors can build a portfolio that not only provides income but also mitigates risk, as these companies tend to be less volatile during market fluctuations.

Another crucial strategy is ESG investing, which emphasizes the importance of environmental, social, and governance factors in selecting investments. Companies that score well on these criteria are often seen as more sustainable and responsible, making them attractive options for investors who prioritize ethical considerations alongside financial returns. This approach not only helps in identifying firms with solid long-term prospects but also aligns with a growing trend among consumers and investors alike, who increasingly favor businesses that contribute positively to society.

Blue-chip stocks also play a significant role in a balanced investment approach. These well-established companies offer reliability and a proven track record of performance, making them a cornerstone for many portfolios. Investors can benefit from their consistent earnings, dividends, and stability, particularly during economic downturns. By investing in blue-chip stocks, investors can enjoy steady capital appreciation and income, which is particularly valuable in uncertain market conditions.

Real Estate Investment Trusts (REITs) represent another attractive opportunity, providing a way to invest in real estate without the direct ownership of property. REITs typically offer high dividend yields and can serve as a hedge against inflation. They can provide consistent income with lower volatility compared to traditional stocks, making them a compelling option for income-focused investors. Moreover, REITs can diversify a portfolio, adding an additional layer of protection against market downturns.

Lastly, the concept of Growth at a Reasonable Price (GARP) allows investors to blend growth investing with value principles. This strategy involves identifying stocks that are undervalued yet poised for growth, striking a balance between potential upside and risk management. By adopting this approach, investors can take advantage of promising companies while maintaining a focus on valuation, ensuring a thoughtful selection process. In conjunction with other strategies such as sector rotation and low-volatility ETFs, investors can craft a diversified portfolio that is well-positioned to thrive in the evolving market landscape of 2025.

Building a Resilient Investment Portfolio

Building a resilient investment portfolio in 2025 requires a multifaceted approach that balances risk and reward across various asset classes. Investors need to consider integrating strategies that focus on low-risk, high-yield opportunities, particularly in the evolving landscape of technology, energy, and sustainable investments. One of the cornerstones of a resilient portfolio is the inclusion of Dividend Aristocrats. These are established companies known for their history of increasing dividends consistently over time. By investing in firms with strong balance sheets and reliable cash flows, investors can enjoy steady income while minimizing risk, making them a foundational component of a low-risk strategy.

Another essential aspect of portfolio construction is ESG investing, which emphasizes environmentally and socially responsible companies. This approach not only reflects a growing consumer preference for sustainability but also tends to align with lower-risk investments as these companies are often better positioned to manage regulatory and reputational risks. By focusing on firms that adhere to ESG principles, investors can tap into solid returns while contributing positively to society. This dual benefit makes ESG stocks an appealing choice for those looking to build a resilient portfolio in 2025.

In addition to ESG stocks, blue-chip stocks offer a reliable option for investors seeking stability and performance. These companies are typically leaders in their industries, possessing a proven track record of financial performance and operational reliability. By including blue-chip stocks in a portfolio, investors can enhance their resilience against market volatility, as these companies are less susceptible to economic downturns. Furthermore, their strong dividends provide a cushion during challenging times, making them an integral part of a low-risk investment strategy.

Real Estate Investment Trusts (REITs) also play a crucial role in a balanced portfolio, offering consistent income with lower volatility. REITs provide exposure to the real estate market without the challenges of direct property ownership. They typically pay high dividends, making them attractive for income-seeking investors. By diversifying into REITs, investors can hedge against stock market fluctuations and benefit from the stability of real estate, further enhancing portfolio resilience.

Lastly, adopting a Growth at a Reasonable Price (GARP) strategy can help investors identify undervalued stocks poised for growth. This approach combines the principles of growth investing with value investing to find companies that are not only growing but are also priced attractively. Additionally, focusing on low-volatility ETFs can provide exposure to stocks with lower price fluctuations, fostering a more stable portfolio. By implementing these diverse strategies, investors can build a resilient investment portfolio that balances high yield with low risk, positioning themselves effectively for the opportunities that 2025 presents.

Future Outlook for Low-Risk High-Yield Investments

The future outlook for low-risk high-yield investments in 2025 presents a promising landscape for investors across various sectors.

As market dynamics evolve, strategies such as focusing on Dividend Aristocrats will remain pivotal. These companies, with a proven history of increasing dividends, offer stability and reliability even in fluctuating markets. Investors are encouraged to identify these long-standing firms, as their commitment to rewarding shareholders can provide a buffer against economic uncertainties while delivering consistent returns.

ESG investing is gaining momentum and is expected to shape investment decisions significantly in the coming years. As more investors prioritize environmental and social responsibility, companies that align with these principles are likely to attract capital. Investing in ESG-compliant firms not only reflects a commitment to sustainability but also positions investors to capitalize on the growing demand for ethical investing. This trend suggests that companies demonstrating strong ESG performance could offer solid returns with comparatively lower risks, making them attractive options for future portfolios.

Blue-chip stocks will continue to be a cornerstone for low-risk high-yield investing strategies. These established companies, known for their reliability and strong performance, provide a level of assurance that is appealing to risk-averse investors. As the market experiences volatility, blue-chip stocks often serve as safe havens, providing dividends and stability. Investors should focus on identifying blue-chip companies with robust fundamentals and a history of weathering economic downturns, as these stocks can enhance portfolio resilience.

Real Estate Investment Trusts (REITs) will play a crucial role in the future outlook for low-risk investments. With their ability to provide consistent income streams and lower volatility compared to other equities, REITs can be an attractive addition to any investment portfolio. As the real estate market continues to evolve, investors should explore various types of REITs, including those focused on residential, commercial, and specialized sectors. This diversification can help mitigate risks while providing opportunities for steady returns.

Lastly, adopting a Growth at a Reasonable Price (GARP) strategy will be essential for identifying undervalued stocks poised for growth. By combining growth investing with value principles, investors can uncover opportunities that offer both appreciation potential and income. Additionally, incorporating low-volatility ETFs into investment strategies can enhance overall portfolio stability. These funds focus on stocks that exhibit lower price fluctuations, providing a balanced approach to achieving steady returns. As investors navigate the complexities of the market, leveraging these strategies will be crucial for achieving success in low-risk high-yield investments in 2025.

www.ingramcontent.com/pod-product-compliance
Lightning Source LLC
Chambersburg PA
CBHW070416230526
45471CB00006B/2836